Oh God...

Oh God...

120 Celebrities' Prayers

Compiled by Steve Chalke

A LION BOOK

Compilation copyright © 1998 Steve Chalke
Prayers © 1998 individual contributors
This edition copyright © 1998 Lion Publishing

Published by
Lion Publishing plc
Sandy Lane West, Oxford, England
www.lion-publishing.co.uk
ISBN 0 7459 4026 9

First edition 1998
10 9 8 7 6 5 4 3 2 1 0

A catalogue record for this book is available
from the British Library

Typeset in 14.25/18 Postcard Alternate
Printed and bound in Great Britain
by Caledonian International Book Manufacturing, Glasgow

Introduction

I've got a cartoon on a pinboard in my office, cut from a newspaper, that pictures a man kneeling at the foot of his bed, praying. Think bubbles rising from his head let you know just what he's praying for.

'More sex, more money. More sex, more money.'

In the next picture, his wife enters the room.

'What are you praying for, darling?' she asks him.

'World peace and an end to global warming,' he replies.

'He's a very special man,' she thinks to herself as she leaves the room.

But the bubbles in the final picture tell a more honest story: 'Now where was I? Oh yes… more sex, more money. More sex, more money.'

We all pray, but most of us keep our *real* prayers to ourselves. Instead of revealing what we actually pray, we opt for telling people what we think we *should* pray.

Only occasionally do we dare to let others hear our real heartfelt requests. Like Augustine, the famous fourth-century saint, who prayed, 'God, make me sexually pure… but not quite yet!'

So, for this book I asked some friends and acquaintances to write down *their* honest prayers. I even asked some people I've never met, but was cheeky enough to approach anyway. The results are sometimes funny, often thought-provoking and always revealing. They take us inside the think bubbles of some of Britain's best-known celebrities.

But not only does this book let you read other people's honest prayers – it lets you *answer* some of them as well. Royalties from its sales are going to Great Ormond Street Hospital, London's famous hospital for children who need long-term or highly specialized medical care.

When he was less than a year old, my son was a patient in Great Ormond Street Hospital. For a while, it was touch and go as to whether or not he'd get well. Today, thanks to the dedication of the staff, he's a healthy teenager. So I know from experience what a wonderful job Great Ormond Street Hospital does, and what a great answer to my prayers it was. By buying this book, you're becoming part of the answer to the prayers of many other parents just like me. So on behalf of all the contributors, who took time out of their busy schedules to pen a prayer, and all those families with children in Great Ormond Street Hospital, a very big thank you.

We hope you enjoy reading *Oh God...* as much as we all enjoyed writing it.

Steve Chalke
London, 1998

Guard all of the good people, kill all of the bad people! That's how you did it in Old Testament times and it seemed to work. Why the change?

Bill Tidy, cartoonist

Dear God,

A short list for you. Sorry, you must get loads. Please can you get:

a pair of world-class defenders for Tottenham (although a pair of small Christmas trees would, frankly, be an improvement);

a lovely girl for my brother (he's starting to worry, you know);

the ability to keep a tidy desk (or tidy anything);

and that gift to see the little bit of yourself you've put in everyone. Can't some people bury it deeply! Thanks.

Simon Mayo

Simon Mayo, DJ and TV presenter

O Lord God,
When grief comes upon us, grant us your comfort.
When loneliness overwhelms us, grant us your presence.
When the day is dark, grant us your light.

Terry Waite

Terry Waite, former Special Envoy for the Archbishop of Canterbury and Beirut hostage

Help me to like crows;
Help me to forgive traffic wardens
and motorists who deafen us with
their mindless music at traffic lights;
Help me to understand what flies are for;
Help me to dislike Chardonnay.

Richard Briers

Richard Briers, actor

Dear God,
I've had more than my share of good luck. So if you had anything to do with it, Why? If you are there... Thanks. If you are not, it's still good to talk to you.

PS: Briers is right about Chardonnay!

John Alderton, actor

Oh God,
What's with the beard?
It looks kinda weird.
Get down the hairdresser's Monday –
You have a day off surely after Sunday?

Harry Hill

Harry Hill, comedian

If it went right: Thank you for today.
If it went wrong: What was I supposed to learn from that?
Please make tomorrow a good hair day with no spots!

Anthea Turner

Anthea Turner, TV presenter

Lord God,
Make my legs move ever faster...
And my path true to your will.
Give me a heart never short of energy...
And growing in love for those around me.
And as I strive for success
Teach me the secret of godly contentment.

Richard Nerurkar

Richard Nerurkar, marathon runner

Dear Creator God,
Since so many of us lay claim to being 'self-made men',
you must be breathing an enormous sigh of relief.

Brian Souter, Chief Executive of Stagecoach

Dear Lord, who knows all the answers but knows I don't, please give me the humility to realize when all I can do for someone is sympathize.

Deidre Sanders

Deirdre Sanders, agony aunt

Oh God,
Please bless politicians with the virtue of total candour...
at least when I am interviewing them.

John Humphrys, journalist and newsreader

Thank you for the gift of communication. Help me to keep my good humour and expression. If only I could transmit in quite the same way that you do.

Bruno Brookes, DJ

Dear God,

Thank you for all the plants and animals that make your world such a wonderful place to be part of. Please help me with my campaign to make the world a safer place for all the products of creative evolution, and to make every child a wanted child.

David Bellamy, educator and environmentalist

God,

I always feel close to you when things are not going so good. I certainly seem to talk to you more then. While I'm in touch, thank you for making my life SO good. Before I go, God, do you think you could improve my golf?

Daniel O'Donnell, singer

Thank you for all the wonderful things in life: our children, our health, our happiness. Please may I ask for just one small thing: that we might *beat* Australia at cricket again — soon!

David Gower, commentator and former England cricketer

Lord,

Give me patience and let me smile more. Look after those I love – and, in angling words, grant me the success of landing a fish so big that even I need not lie in the telling of it.

Fiona Armstrong, television broadcaster and angler

Wounded and helpless within three yards of a Japanese trench in the jungle, I prayed: 'Oh God, please get me out of here!' He did.

John Ryan

John Ryan, cartoonist and creator of 'Captain Pugwash'

Dear God,
Smile on all the children, and whilst you're doing that,
make me a better putter!

Jimmy Tarbuck O.B.E.

Jimmy Tarbuck OBE, comedian and golfer

Lord, when I was in doubt
I always stuck my left out.
Is there anything else?

Henry Cooper, former heavyweight boxing champion

Thank you for making me a man, so that I can appreciate rugby, understand American football, drive at naughty miles per hour round bends and imagine I'm Damon Hill; so that I can go to boxing matches – and even have golfing weekends with Henry Cooper, and not feel guilty. AND... take out the garbage, coax the spiders out of the bath, mop up the dog vomit, get out the drain rods when the loo is blocked...

Oh God, maybe you ARE a woman.

Dickie Davies, sports presenter

Dear God,
Sometimes I wish you hadn't...
but I don't mean it.

Martyn Joseph, singer/songwriter

Thank you for helping me in my hour of need. I will go back to the sea, but I now know that you will be with me. What better crew can I have by my side?

Tony Bullimore

Tony Bullimore, international yachtsman

Why do tragedies happen? Can no one explain? What surely can be happening to this world? Can no one explain? The suffering and the pain that people experience – can no one explain? Hunger, sadness, deprivation and loneliness – who can explain? The only time we will ever know is when God calls us to be with him. Then surely he will explain.

Lisa Potts GM, primary school teacher and hero

Thank you for Laurel & Hardy, the Marx Brothers, Morecambe & Wise and Tommy Cooper. Thank you for making me modest enough not to mention my own name.

Frank Carson, comedian

Thank you for my many blessings and keep me ever mindful of the needs of others.

Liz Earle

Liz Earle, lifestyle guru

Dear God,

It is perfectly clear from history that either you take bugger all notice of people's prayers, or you don't exist. I therefore am not asking you for anything — unless you care to comment on my cynicism?

Bill Oddie, comic and ornithologist

Thank you for giving me the gift of talking my way out of awkward situations. Help me to resist the allure of chips and chocolate biscuits (especially Hob Nobs). Give me the strength to do those pelvic floor exercises. Thanks for letting me inherit my mother's skin tone and legs – although I could have done without my dad's moustache! Oh, and by the way – thanks again for my daughter Rosie!

Lorraine Kelly, TV presenter

Teach me to say, 'Thank you, God' more often,
And 'God, please sort it' rather less.
Help me to stop wanting quite so much,
And to start giving that much more.

Frances Edmonds, author

Help me to know that 'always' means Monday mornings, Board meetings, standing up to give a speech, and the middle of the night, and that always your love for us is right here deep in all our hearts.

Jim Harding, Director and Chief Executive, NSPCC

Please help me to live my life as I would wish to have lived it when I am lying there dying.

Neil 'Doctor' Fox, Capital FM DJ

Oh Lord God,

Thank you for the save against Pele – not just at the time of making it, but it has helped me later on in my life. But PLEASE do me and all elderly people one huge favour: slow down time, oh Lord.

Gordon Banks

Gordon Banks, England 1966 World Cup goalkeeper

Thank you for all the good things that happen in life. But why do you allow so much evil and cruelty? Would it really be so hard for you to endow all of us with the gifts of humanity and compassion?

Angela Rippon

Angela Rippon, TV presenter

When I stumble, pick me up.
When I wander, bring me back.
When I doubt, restore my faith.
When I'm arid, quench my thirst.

David Alton.

Lord Alton of Liverpool

Thank you for giving us our five senses: sight, hearing, touch, smell and taste. Help us to remember that, if we are ever going to succeed in life, we need to develop two more: horse and common. Help us to avoid complaining just because there are thorns among the roses, and always be thankful that you put roses among the thorns.

Mr Motivator, fitness guru

Dear God,

I would like to remember and pray for all the children in the world who have lost a parent. Help them to find peace and to use the memories of an unfinished life to give them strength to face the future.

[signature: Ruth Harding]

Ruth Harding, widow of Chelsea FC vice-chairman Matthew Harding

Thank you for my girls – and girl. Thank you for making me too busy to see them much! But I'm listening, and must retire soon, O God. Please use me more.

Ian McCaskill

Ian McCaskill, former BBC weather presenter

Please help me to be a kinder and more tolerant person.

Bill Beaumont, former England rugby captain

Oh God,
Please let me get through the paperwork on my desk
and the jobs round the house as quickly as possible,
so I can get out into the garden.

Penelope Keith, actress

Oh God, could this be the day?

Michael Aspel, TV presenter

Oh God,
Please help me to stop, think, take a breath and remember what I've got, rather than what I want. Maybe then I'll be a little easier to live with!

Sally Meen

Sally Meen, TV and radio presenter

Here we go again... Please be there.

Alvin Stardust, signer

Alvin Stardust, singer

Please let the salmon bite, the hole-in-one be not too far off, England be top of the sporting nations. Not too much to ask, is it?

Ian Botham, former England cricketer

Help me to understand what I don't understand,
but when I can't, I know you do.

Beechy Colclough, psychiatrist

Lord,

Give me the strength and the ability to help and support as many people as I can. Thank you for loving and supporting me every second of every minute of every hour of every day, all of my life.

Rosemary Conley, fitness guru

Give me the humour to grow old gracefully and the wisdom to know that's what I'm doing.

PS: If life is meant to teach us, why did you invent senility? So that we can forget it all and come back for more next time?

Jenny Seagrove, actress

Please help me to remember to do unto others as I would see done unto me. And thank you for all the good in life, and for giving me the power to make it better.

Sharron Davies, former Olympic swimming champion

Oh God,
Help me to remember that people will judge me by their standards, that I will judge others by my standards, and that you will judge me by your standards.

[signature: John Stapleton]

John Stapleton, TV presenter

My greatest dread on an expedition is losing someone — I've lost all too many friends on trips in the past. Oh God, let them get back down alive and well.

C. Bonington

Sir Chris Bonington, mountaineer, praying for the safety of his team

When I say, 'I'm drinking just one glass of wine and no more,' can you convince me that I mean it? When I say, 'No, thank you, I don't smoke,' can you convince me that I mean it? When I say, 'I'd be at the gym every day, if only I had the time,' can you convince me that I mean it? And when I say, 'Thank you for my family, and for making me so lucky in life,' I don't need convincing – I mean it!

Fiona Phillips

Fiona Phillips, TV presenter

Please listen to what I ask for, but give me what YOU know I need. Please help me to develop my talent, but in the way that YOU want it used.

Rick Wakeman, former YES keyboard player

Dear God,
Please help me to keep my sense of humour
when cack happens!

Joe Pasquale, comedian

Thank you for the blessings of good health, and the pleasure that brings. Thank you for the blessing of children, and the joy they give. Sustain the needy, comfort the afflicted and, above all, bring enlightenment to those who are disturbed or sick in mind, so the world may be a safer and happier place for everyone.

Nicholas Parsons, radio and TV presenter

Thank you for another day,
And for guiding me along the way.
Thank you for being there when I need an ear,
And for helping me overcome any fear.
Thank you for blessing me with dear friends,
And for the love and affection that people send.
Thank you for letting me Carry On in Albert Square,
And for listening to my little prayer.

Barbara Windsor signature

Barbara Windsor, actress

God,
I thank you for the gift of humour to celebrate human happiness and all that makes us glad. We give thanks also for the gift of laughter as we share in the joy of creation and especially in your exuberant self-giving in Jesus Christ our Lord. Give us all grateful hearts.

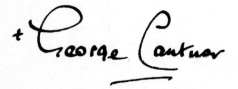

George Carey, Archbishop of Canterbury

Help me to be less like me and more like you.

Tony Holland

Tony Holland, TV muscle-man and unbeaten *Opportunity Knocks* winner

Dear God...
Please, please, please can I go through a whole day
without breaking a single bone in my body?

Chris Tarrant, DJ and TV presenter

Thank you for... everything — my family, my friends, my lifestyle, my computer.

PS: Can you do PSs, because there's always something I forget?

Andi Peters, TV presenter

Thank you for giving us all different skills and talents...
Whatever it is we have, dear Lord, help us to use it
in a caring way for the service of others – and so in
serving them we can show our love for you as our Saviour
and Lord.

Brian Irvine, footballer

O Lord,
Make the audience like me... but if not, please
give me a hundred yards' start!

Sir Harry Secombe, 'Goon'

Help me to remember you when I am happy,
And when I'm not, remind me of how wonderful my life is.

Barbara Dickson, actress and singer

Help me always to remember your teachings in the Sermon on the Mount, and especially those that I find so difficult to put into practice. When I am driving in traffic, I so often find someone wishes to treat me as their enemy by cutting me up, or driving dangerously close. Help me to love my enemies! Teach me patience and care and when, if they continue driving like this, they have the accident that they unconsciously seek, may it be serious enough to teach them a lesson without causing bodily harm to anyone.

Maurice Laing

Sir Maurice Laing, industrialist

Please help me get up earlier in the mornings and not go to bed quite so late. Please help me like fruit and veg and healthy foods as much as I like chocolate. Please help me bite my tongue when dealing with bureaucrats, jobsworths and petty-minded pen-pushers. Please help me regard computers as a friend rather than an enemy. And if you can manage it, please help me improve my skiing!

Siân Lloyd

Siân Lloyd, ITN weather correspondent

A grace I once heard during a meeting of
the Commonwealth Parliamentary Association:

Lord, make me not like porridge: heavy and hard to stir.
Make me rather like cornflakes: quick and ready to serve.

Roger Gale, MP

Thank you for everything you have given me and help me to concentrate more on what you've given and less on what I think I haven't got. And if you could pull a few more strings in the War on World Hunger department, I'd be happy. I've never heard a good explanation for hunger yet. Finally, Lord, can you help me cut down on my use of the word 'me'? Thanks for listening, and I'll see you in the morning.

Matthew Lorenzo

Matthew Lorenzo, TV presenter

I shall pass through this world but once. Any good therefore that I can do, or any kindness that I can show to any human being, let me do it now. Let me not defer or neglect, for I shall not pass this way again.

Faith Brown, comedienne and Margaret Thatcher impersonator

Don't give up on us. This is no time to retire.

Leslie Thomas, cricketer

I know that when a door is closed to me, you always open at least a window. But please make sure it's a French window!

Patti Boulaye, singer

A prayer I made up as a little boy, when I used to sleep with my teddy bear on my tummy in case I got stabbed:

Dear God,
Make no one get murdered, killed or die tonight, and make everyone have no bad dreams, no nightmares, just peaceful dreams tonight, Lord.

Frazer Hines, actor

Help me to understand better. Just when I think things are going well, everything goes belly up; help me understand why. When a horse is trying to cart me across a field, help me understand why I'm there at all.

When I think I'm so happy and suddenly I'm sad,
When Frazer won't pick up his socks and suddenly I'm mad,
Help me understand, dear Lord, why you try me so,
When all I really want is peace and for our love to grow.

Liz Hobbs MBE, TV presenter and former world water-ski champion, married to Frazer Hines

I'm sure you are happy, great and droll.
Please show my nine where is the goal.
As I get older, you get nearer,
Is there any chance of Alan Shearer?

Lawrie McMenemy

Lawrie McMenemy, football manager

Dear God in heaven above,
Please look after all those I love;
Help me to keep my health,
And steer me to do right,
And oh! What about a win for United
By three goals tonight!

Eamonn Holmes, TV presenter and Manchester United supporter

Oh God,
I wonder if you could do something (without killing
too many people) to get the human race to look after
each other a bit better, and cherish the planet earth
at the same time. It's not much to ask.

Hilary Jones, doctor and TV presenter

I thank you for all the good things in my life. I ask for your help in overcoming any problems I or my family may have. I praise you and glorify you. I ask you to forgive my sins and help me to follow you always.

Bryan Mosley

Bryan Mosley, 'Alf Roberts' in *Coronation Street*

On the end of my everyday talk with God comes:

I would like to pray for the peace and happiness of everybody — the living, the dead and especially those who are troubled, poorly, or a victim, that sometime today they could feel terrific for a while.

Sir Jimmy Savile, philanthropist and former DJ

God, which is beyond both my understanding and my experience but which I believe to be the life in me and all things, allow me to know it. Remove my fear of faith, enlighten me, and let me delight in your presence in me.

Peter Skellern, singer/songwriter

One thing I know, life can never die,
Translucent, splendid, flaming like the sun.
Only our bodies wither and deny
The life force when our strength is done.
Let me transmit this wonderful fire,
Even a little through my heart and mind,
Bringing the perfect love we all desire
To those who seek, yet blindly cannot find.

Dame Barbara Cartland, author

Sometimes I feel a long way from you. A bit like the Prodigal Son in a faraway country. Help me to see past my feelings and personal circumstances, and to trust you so that I may be effective in everything I do for you today.

Kriss Akabusi

Kriss Akabusi MBE, Olympic champion and TV presenter

Thank you for always being there and never sleeping. 'You're the Rock that doesn't roll.'

Tommy Cannon

Tommy Cannon, comedian

I don't ask for material things,
Lots of clothes or even money.
It's just that when I have to go on stage
Please God, make me funny!

Bobby Ball, comedian

Thank you for helping me transform the wilderness that was my garden into a beautiful display of lawns and flower beds. Between us we have worked wonders.

PS: You should have seen the garden when you had it all to yourself!

Rod Hull

Rod Hull, entertainer

Dear God,

You know when, for the umpteenth time in one single day, I chastise myself for being slovenly, greedy or grumpy? Could you please just give me an electric shock so I stop thinking about this predicament and actually do something to change myself for the better? Thank you. I'm sorry to bother you.

Toyah Willcox, actress, singer and *Teletubbies* voice

Oh God,
It would help if you gave the umpire back his sight,
and assisted him to raise his finger when I next appeal.

Trevor Bailey, cricket all-rounder

Help me do right, do well, and do what I promise.

Tom Watt, actor and football fanatic

'Thank you, God, for the blessings of this day, and please keep us all safe this night 'til morning light'... to which my daughter Katie's frequent reply is, 'And thank you, God, for guinea-pigs.'

Carol Vorderman, TV presenter

May I thank you, O Lord, and of course your dear Father,
For the help in my lonely, sad childhood palaver.
I was homeless and hungry, often sleeping in ditches,
Then fate steered me slowly from rags to some riches...
My thanks to you, God, are honestly true.
You've made me so happy with all that I do.
In fact, my thoughts are now so sincere,
That, looking back, I can still shed a tear.

Norman Wisdom

Norman Wisdom, actor

Help me to remember that you made all the things that I reckon are dangerous. They are therefore under control and not out to get me.

Sir Ranulph Fiennes, adventurer

O good Lord, who didst turn water into wine,
Deliver us from evil men who would turn it back again!

Colonel John Blashford-Snell, expedition leader

Dear Lord,

I pray that I won't let anyone down, but if this audience doesn't like me, please show me the nearest exit and give me the strength to run fast!

Tim Vine, stand-up comedian

Oh Lord,
It does not matter whose God you think you are;
please, just help me!

Bill Morris, General Secretary, T&G

Thank you, Lord, for pigeons on wickets.
Thank you, Lord, for dogs and crickets.
Thank you, Lord, for days of sun.
Thank you, Lord, for friends and fun.
Thank you, Lord, that you made me me
(And not someone else).

Dickie Bird, cricket umpire

Thank you, God, for the gift of grandchildren;
I love them to come and stay.
And thank you, God, for that blessed peace
That descends when they've gone away.

Jean Crowther

Jean Crowther, widow of Leslie Crowther

Help me to be gentler on myself.

Alan Titchmarsh, green-fingered TV presenter

For health and strength and daily bread
We sing thy praise, Almighty.
If we smile at a sinner,
Give the hungry our dinner,
We can all view the future more brightly.

Kevin Woodford, TV chef

Mrs Patrick Campbell's heartfelt theatrical prayer, on her knees in her dressing room before a performance:

Please God, make George Howe a good actor.

Peter Sallis, 'Clegg' in Last of the Summer Wine and voice of 'Wallace' in Wallace and Gromit

Help me to be kinder to people who really get up my nose, and less scared of getting involved in helping others. Please keep my children safe and healthy – and keep the blighters asleep ALL night tonight. Thank you, God, for always being there for me and for everyone.

Fern Britton, presenter of *Ready, Steady, Cook*

Why have I not yet achieved a hole-in-one at golf?
But my deep faith in you says, 'I will...'

F.S. Trueman

Freddie Trueman OBE, former England cricketer

Give me the wisdom to remember that ninety per cent of the stuff I worry about goes away of its own accord, and the strength to deal with the ten per cent that doesn't.

Ross Kelly, TV presenter

When I'm faced with sadness, thank you for helping me to remember all the good there is in this world, and especially how fortunate I am. Thank you for all that I feel. You have given me the power to question, a mouth to speak, and eyes and heart with which to cry – and smile. And amongst all this you have given me hope, trivial as it may seem, that I shall never gain weight despite the huge amounts of chocolate I might consume!

Diane Louise Jordan, TV presenter

Do you doubt me as much as I doubt you?
Somehow, I doubt it.

Peter Krysowski

Peter Krysowski, film producer

Help me to be less impetuous, more tolerant and
a nicer man. If you could make me be more the way
I would like other people to be, I am sure I'd be fine.
Maybe rather a lot of us need your help!

Stirling Moss, former champion racing driver

A prayer by E.Y. Harburg, lyricist for *The Wizard of Oz*:

No matter how much I probe and prod,
I cannot quite believe in God;
But oh, I hope to God that he
Unswervingly believes in me.

Ned Sherrin, broadcaster and raconteur

Thank you for giving me a talent to earn my living by talking to myself... when most people would be locked up!

Keith Harris, ventriloquist and duck minder

Please make Keith cut his nails.

Orville

It is a competitive world and the pressure to succeed is great: please give me a sense of perspective. Help me to be more concerned about impressing you than other people; and to stick to the task when faced with things I do not like having to do.

Christopher Martin-Jenkins, sports commentator

At times, give me the strength to hush my tongue,
Especially when others think I should be 'done'.
Silence was never my strongest force,
But as I get older, it could be my greatest resource.

Gloria Hunniford, Radio 2 DJ

Thank you for our daily weather, which continues to astound me even after half a century. The beauty of a summer's day, the frightening dark of a thunderstorm: they all show your vision. But I still wish you would take responsibility for the 1987 storm!

Bill Giles

Bill Giles, Head of BBC Weather Centre

They say that you work in mysterious ways,
And that would explain why I can't get a raise.
But sometimes I doubt that you're watching over me:
If you were, it'd surely be 'SIMON's House Party'!
So, God, if you're there, please give me a sign...
Five balls and the bonus, now that'd do fine.

Simon Parkin, TV presenter

As one of Nelson's admirals prayed just before the battle of Trafalgar:

'Oh God,
Tomorrow I shall be very busy. I may forget about you, but do not thou forget about me!'

Tom O'Connor, comedian

Please don't let me pull my hamstring now!

Gareth Edwards, former Welsh rugby captain, en route to scoring the first try for the 1973 Barbarians v. New Zealand match

Your Bible tells us to 'Fight the good fight of faith' and 'Finish the race'. Perhaps promoting boxing events is not such a bad business to be in after all! The 'finishing the race' part is rather more tricky — avoiding gunshots and that... So please keep my family and business in your care and safety. Thank you.

Frank Warren, boxing promoter

I know you take pity on those who suffer. My suffering has gone on for many years now, and at times it does seem that there is no light at the end of the tunnel. Please God, have mercy on this humble sinner and help Fulham get into the Premier League!

David Hamilton, TV presenter and DJ

Yesterday is a memory, tomorrow is a mystery, and today is a gift – that's why they call it 'the present'. Thank you, God, for the best gift of all: life.

Linda Nolan

Linda Nolan, singer

As the whole sun is reflected
in each raindrop on the trees
after a storm, so your care
reaches every member of your family,
O Lord. Help us to live together
in the peace of your eternal love.

Cicely

Dame Cicely Saunders OM, DBE, FRCP, founder/chairman of St Christopher's Hospice, London

Please stop me enjoying chocolate cakes.
Please stop me drinking Cointreau,
because it brings on a migraine.
Please help me stick to a diet.
Please let me understand things my accountant tells me.
Please let me carry on living a happy life.
Please let my children be as happy as I have been.

Cheryl Baker

Cheryl Baker, TV presenter and former member of *Buck's Fizz*

You have always been there for me; I have not always been there for you — yet you still guide my footsteps through life. Give me the grace to remember this always and give thanks for it.

Oh — thank you for giving me the most wonderful, loyal, strong, dedicated and loving wife a man could wish for. I know she is your instrument.

Roger Whittaker, singer/songwriter

Life is full of obstacles. When an obstacle seems too high to climb, help me find another way to get around, under or through it.

Chrystal Rose, TV presenter

God, you're good; God, you're true;
I can always be sure of you.
God, you're good; God, you're divine;
I am always on a very thin line.
God, you're good; God, you're the master;
You are better than any plaster.
God, you're good; God, you're almighty;
You won't scare me in my nightie.

Sam Torrance, golfer

Please help me to steer clear of sloppy eaters who talk with their mouths full and spit their food all over you; of thoughtless and discourteous drivers; of people who are rude, cruel and selfish. And please give great happiness to people who are unselfish, who care for the ill and the dying. Please keep the flowers growing in my garden and in the hedgerows.

Judith Chalmers

Judith Chalmers, TV presenter

We all need a helping hand.
Help us to learn to help each other.

Peter André, singer

I'm truly sorry for giving my husband David such a hard time when he was teaching me to drive. He's not such a bad driver, I suppose. Sometimes I'd like to swap him, but I'm grateful for him really.

MaD Mo Ree

Mo Rees, star of *Driving School*

Please God,
Let my children love me as much when they
are teenagers as when they were toddlers.

Pauline Quirke

Pauline Quirke, 'Sharon' in *Birds of a Feather*

Acknowledgments

Thank you to all those who responded to my pestering, in spite of their hectic diaries, and sent in a prayer. Thanks also to Hugh Faupel, who encouraged this idea; to Maurice Lyon, who adopted it; and to all those at Oasis Media, especially Heather Hookway and Charlotte Mungeam, who did so much of the legwork to make it happen.